Up Consumer Creek Without a Paddle: Take Control Before You Go Under

By G. B. Taken

PUBLISHED BY GB TAKEN

Copyright Year: 2010
Copyright Notice: by GB Taken. All rights reserved.
The above information forms this copyright notice: © 2010 by GB Taken. All rights reserved.
ISBN: 978-1-304-30061-4
Printed in the United States of America
January 2010
First Edition

Dedication

To all the consumers who have went "up the creek".

Table of Contents

Up Consumer Creek Without A Paddle…

All The Presidents' Plans…

Foreclosure Rescue, Credit Repair And Debt Settlement Scams…

Consumer Rights And A Few Things I Have Learned: For The Most Desperate…

Credit Card Questions…

Debtors Make Bankruptcy Decision Without Facts Of Mortgage…

FDIC Myths and Reality: How Safe is Your Money…

Fighting The Zombie Banks…

Have a Plan: Foreclosure And Your Pets…

Half Of Banks Can't Prove They Own Mortgages…

How the Courts Fail You Everyday…

How To Hire A Lawyer To Save Your Home…

How To Stop Foreclosure…

Mortgage Nightmares to Learn From…

More Mortgage Nightmares to Learn From…

Ninety Percent Of Borrowers Are Unhappy With Their Mortgage Servicer…

Sins Of The Mortgage Servicer…

When You Can't Trust Bankers…

Who Really Owns Your Home?…

Questions and Answers
Question 1…
Question 2…
Question 3…
Question 4…
Question 5…
Question 6…

Question 7…
Question 8…
Question 9…
Question 10…
Question 11…
Question 12…

Up Consumer Creek Without A Paddle

It is every family for themselves and the odds are increasingly against them. We are all being swept up in the current and stench that is Consumer Creek. Ahoy! And good luck to all that shoot the rapids.

The decades of extreme lending and spending that had banks providing loans for everyone and everything short of paperboys and tree houses has come tumbling down like a house of cards. The cycle of destruction continues; lending is frozen, foreclosures continue, unemployment is on the rise, companies once thought to be permanent fixtures are in jeopardy of being closed down.

The banking system is rotten to the core; it cannot be fixed and should be left to die and rebuilt anew. Insurance companies having dabbled in the financial voodoo as well, are fearful of insolvency and will be the next to face these problems and potentially collapse.

Folks with credit lines smashed, cars repossessed and in fear of foreclosure will be left to litter the countryside. The consumer landscape will be different after this economic storm ends and no one really knows when this will be. Not since the 1930's have Americans encountered such an economic disruption. We are entering into a consumer dark age that threatens to destroy homeownership, the middle class and family stability itself.

Survival is the only thing that counts when you find yourself up the creek without a paddle. It is literally where the "tough get going" and the not so tough are devoured by the monsters from the bottom of the creek. The issue of survival has everything to do with how you react to your problems; will it be a matter of fight or flight?

Half of the battle is making sure your creditors have the details of your accounts correct and are following the law throughout the transaction. The other half of the challenge is you, as a consumer, must change your ways. Your best defense is to spend less and save more.

We must be adults and take ownership of our decisions and actions, it means being responsible. Responsibility is a two way street in that the consumer providing the demand and the corporation providing the product or service both conduct themselves in reliable ways. Your life will change when you carefully consider each and every transaction you make. It will be a life-changing experience for your creditors as well when you make them be accountable for an accurate and honest handling of your business.

Millions of families will never return from their turbulent journey up Consumer Creek. Many economists fear a forthcoming depression; some argue we are already there. We must take it upon ourselves to be defined as something other than a consumer, just get out of the canoe, and stand on solid ground.

All The Presidents' Plans

The housing collapse of recent years has produced a number of responses by both the Bush and Obama Administrations. The most common complaint about these programs is that they don't assist those who are unemployed or too far behind in payments. There are other shortfalls as well.

The Hope Now alliance initiated by the Bush team has proven to be severely limited in who can qualify. HOPE NOW was a joint effort by HUD approved counseling agents, mortgage companies, investors and other mortgage market participants to provide free foreclosure prevention assistance.

Created in 2007, proponents of the idea claim it has assisted 1 million homeowners. The objective was to allow folks to reach an agreement on a repayment schedule or if this was not possible a loan modification. The problem is it was left to the discretion of mortgage companies if they wanted to participate or not.

The Hope Now Program is recommending several loan programs. Project Lifeline targets homeowners that are delinquent 90-days or more. Six HOPE NOW alliance members that are servicers will begin the program by providing a letter to seriously delinquent homeowners offering a simple "step-by-step" approach that, if followed, may enable them to "pause" their foreclosure for 30 days while a potential loan modification is evaluated.

Project Lifeline includes only a half dozen of America's largest lenders more interested, as was the Bush Administration, in appearance than substance. This plan, like all the others offered by both the government and the banks, has been criticized as ineffective window dressing.

Another program offered by the Hope Now counselors is the HOPE for Homeowners (H4H) program that was created by Congress to help those at risk of default and foreclosure to refinance into more affordable, sustainable loans. The program will be in effect from October 1, 2008 through September 30, 2011. For borrowers who refinance under HOPE for Homeowners, lenders will be required to "write down" the size of the mortgage to a maximum of 90 percent of the home's new appraised value. HOPE for Homeowners will only offer 30-year, fixed rate mortgages. To qualify your mortgage must have originated on or before January 1, 2008.

The Federal Housing Authority's FHASecure program offers refinancing options to help delinquent ARM borrowers get reasonable, fixed-rate loans. FHASecure targets owners whose mortgages have gone delinquent due to the increase in payments after interest rates have reset. Since that doesn't happen for at least two years for most hybrid ARM loans, those written after December 31, 2006 will not qualify for the program.

The Making Home Affordable Program President Obama started will help you refinance if you are a homeowner who is current on your mortgage payments but unable to refinance to a lower interest rate because your home value has decreased. The most recent "foreclosure remedy" introduced by the new administration also offers more incentives to banks to become involved.

If you are a homeowner who is current on your mortgage payments but unable to refinance to a lower interest rate because your home value has decreased, you may be able to refinance.

For a loan refinance:

- ? You must be the owner of a one- to four-unit home;
- ? You must be current on your mortgage payments; "Current" means that you haven't been more than 30-days late on your mortgage payment in the last 12 months;
- ? You believe that the amount you owe on your first mortgage is about the same or less than the current value of your house.

For a loan modification:

- ? They got a mortgage before January 1, 2009;
- ? Having trouble making payments on time;
- ? The amount you owe on your first mortgage equal to or less than $729,750;

- Payment on your first mortgage (including principal, interest, taxes, insurance and homeowner's association dues, if applicable) is more than 31% of your current gross income.

Many housing advocates believe these actions are still not as substantial as the foreclosure crisis demands. If you are too far behind in payments or your house has depreciated in value beyond the threshold then you don't qualify.

With the increase in unemployment and foreclosure threatening homeownership and the middleclass itself, more drastic measures may be needed. Many experts believe a foreclosure moratorium that suspends all foreclosures for six months or one year is needed to stop the snowball effect taking place.

Whether or not these programs will help remains to be seen. If you are waiting on any legislation aimed at curbing the majority of foreclosures to an absolute minimum; don't hold your breath. A complete overhaul as well as regulation of an irresponsible and corrupt banking system is required in order to save homeownership.

Foreclosure Rescue, Credit Repair And Debt Settlement Scams

There is a particularly parasitic swarm of fraudsters feeding upon vulnerable consumers in search of help. As foreclosure threatens and bankruptcy looms, millions of Americans are at risk of falling prey to scammers that will bilk them of much needed cash resources and leave them worse off for using bogus credit repair and foreclosure rescue services.

Many debtors are devastated by these bloodsuckers and oftentimes lose their homes. Financial burdens are the leading cause of divorce and family collapse. All the more reason why to carefully consider your options.

When you are in a financial crisis it is easy to make mistakes regarding where to turn for assistance and what to do to solve your problems. Even when we should have known better, in light of a more dubious offer, we may suspend our disbelief because the idea of easing or curing our debt-load is appealing, even lifesaving.

Consumers would do themselves a great favor if they held any company offering services that promise to stop a foreclosure, repair credit or negotiate debt with all the suspicion and contempt they would have for a homicidal maniac. It is important to be alert for those offering services or "protections" that only a bankruptcy court has the authority to give you, or peddling services never delivered, while charging you fees and assuring you all the while that all will be okay.

Be alert for shady foreclosure rescue businesses trying to get possession of your property. It is a common occurrence for companies like this to charge up-front fees for "counseling" and additional charges are incurred for the company to negotiate on a homeowner's behalf with the mortgage company. Some homeowners send money to such organizations believing these funds will go to satisfy outstanding debt. The problem is payments are never made and negotiations never happen and the consumer is left to the merciless creditors and even further in the hole.

Things Scammers Do

- Advise you not to pay your bills.
- Charge you upfront fees.
- Attempt to steal your deed.
- Falsely advertise as a nonprofit.
- Promise to erase debt at a third of the cost of the entire debt.
- Offer useless, even dangerous advice.
- Lure you into a false sense of confidence that something is being done to resolve your problems. In reality, you are being ripped-off while your debt increases, as does your creditors' impatience.

Even if your creditors are taking an abusive or tough stand, remember to be cordial and keep in contact with all of them. My experience has taught me that given the opportunity to abuse you, a creditor will do just that. It is vitally important to correspond with all of your creditors in writing. Doing so will give you the capability to file complaints to regulators, pursue abuses in a civil court and establish evidence that could void a creditor's ability to file a claim and collect in a bankruptcy court.

Regardless of how thuggish your creditors behave, there are laws mortgage companies and collection agencies must follow. Before you are pushed into an ever-increasing desperate situation, consult some real experts about your consumer rights. Use the free visit or consultation lawyers offer in your area.

Don't let the gangsters at the bank get you stressed or depressed, there are alternatives. While fighting my bad bankers for six years in a civil suit my payments were suspended and if you have to exercise your rights, your payments may be suspended as well. The most useful things revealed during my lawsuit were; my bankers had committed lots of fraud and the bank trying to foreclose on me could not produce a mortgage note or a legal deed of trust. This is more common than you would think.

If you insist on trying your luck with questionable companies offering consumer assistance, check with the attorney general in your state to see what they think of your idea to engage such entities. Also, check with the Better Business Bureau for any complaints they may have on record. Remember, if it is too good to be true…

Consumer Rights And A Few Things I Have Learned: For The Most Desperate

As the economy continues to tank and creditors turn up the heat on consumers already at the boiling point, we will unfortunately hear many horrific stories of people pushed beyond the brink. Millions of Americans are losing their jobs, cars, homes; their cash resources are nonexistent and their credit lines are closed. The very security that is essential to a family is eroding and divorce is a common result.

Fear and loathing continue to build until many lose control and resort to violence upon themselves and/or family members. No one ever thinks these things will happen to their family. It happens everyday as creditors threaten foreclosure and practice an array of abusive collection methods that pressures people, distorts rational judgment and leaves debtors as an exposed raw nerve.

If you are dealing with a bad bank acting in a predatory manner, facing foreclosure and fearing you may lose everything, take a moment to realize it is not the end. For instance, in my own situation the bank tried to strong-arm me and I filed a civil suit. During the lawsuit that lasted six years, I was not required to make monthly payments and all of the bank's earlier threats faded as I realized I had an ace in the hole, no matter how incompetent my attorney. The bank had no enforceable lien and the same is true for literally millions of homeowners.

Regardless of the type of thug that is bullying you for whatever bill, just remember they have to follow the rules or as some of us like to call it, the law. Creditors can be some of the fiercest pack of bastards; lying, vicious and even criminal behavior is standard operating procedure. Banks and other institutions regularly break numerous laws while bringing you the nightmarish service and collection threats. Don't let them push you around, companies have to obey the law, many do not.

Consumer credit transactions are regulated both at the federal and the state level. Some of the federal laws influencing the credit industry are:

Federal Laws

- Bankruptcy Reform Act of 1978
- Helping Families Save Their Homes in Bankruptcy Act of 2009
- Consumer Leasing Act
- Equal Credit Opportunity Act
- Fair Credit Billing Act
- Fair Credit Reporting Act
- Fair Debt Collection Practices Act
- Federal Consumer Credit Protection Act
- Right to Financial Privacy Act
- Truth in Lending Act
- RESPA
- Unsolicited Credit Act

While there is considerable variation among state laws governing consumer credit transactions, most are based on federal laws and versions of other state laws relating to standard areas of consumer protection. Here are some examples:

State Laws

- Consumer loan acts
- Home improvement contracts acts

- Home solicitation sales acts
- Mortgage banker and broker acts
- Mortgage lending acts
- Retail installment sales acts
- Rental purchase agreement acts
- Secondary mortgage acts
- Seller and lender credit card acts
- Usury or rate ceiling laws

The Helping Families Save Their Homes in Bankruptcy Act of 2009 allows judges to modify the terms of a mortgage. It is hoped that this will give options to homeowners that did not exist prior to this act. There are new credit card laws that are to go into effect as of July 1, 2010, which will prohibit creditors from readjusting your rates without notice. This reform is aimed at stopping two-cycle billing schemes and other abusive practices used to take advantage of a cardholder.

Don't Wait Until the Last Minute

Before you let the stress build or your creditors run roughshod over you, find the support or counseling you and your family may need. First and foremost find an attorney to examine your situation to determine if a suit must be filed. This act alone will give much needed time and breathing room. For other support, contact your church or local outreach for professional stress-management counseling.

Credit Card Questions

Question: How do the new credit card laws protect me and when do they go into effect?

Answer: The new regulations focus primarily on banning certain types of interest rate hikes and late fees. For instance, a credit card company will no longer be allowed to raise a cardholder's interest rate on an existing balance if that cardholder is paying on time.

The new laws are supposed to make it easier for a consumer to repay his or her debt. Billing statements must be sent 21 days before the due date, giving you more time to pay your credit card bill and reducing the risk of a late fee and interest rate penalty. Furthermore, credit card companies will no longer be allowed to take advantage of the payment system in a way that shakes down the cardholder for maximum profits for the creditor. The new credit card rules go into effect July 1, 2010..

Question: Do the new laws going into effect in 2010 ban "universal default"?

Answer: "Universal default" is the oppressive and pervasive practice that credit card companies use to raise a cardholder's interest rate due to a seemingly arbitrary combination of reasons. Your credit card company may raise your rates if you open other lines of credit, if you are late on a utility bill or your credit score takes a dive. It is an abuse creditors heap on their customers "at any time for any reason." The new rules regulate but do not prohibit this practice.

Credit card companies can no longer increase your interest rate in the first year of service or without a forty-five day notice. It is not a very effective "reform" our nation's lawmakers have given us. It seems hardly worth the effort. You will want to look into your own state's laws, several states are banning universal default yours may be one. Check your state's consumer code to see if there are any provisions that may protect you against such practices.

Question: Is it true there is no limit to how high an interest rate my credit card company can charge. My state has laws banning this very thing. How can the credit card companies get away with this?

Answer: In *Marquette vs. First Omaha Service Corp.*, the Supreme Court ruled that a national bank could charge the highest interest rate allowed in their home state to customers living anywhere in the United States, this includes states with laws capping interest rates. This is exactly how credit card companies get away with this; thanks, Supreme Court for nothing.

Question: Can my credit card company cut my credit limit without warning?

Answer: While the rules of 2010 makes it mandatory to give a cardholder a 45-day notice of an interest rate increase no such law has been provided to ban a creditor from reducing your card limit without forewarning.

Debtors Make Bankruptcy Decision Without Facts Of Mortgage

As tens of thousands of Americans file Chapter 13 each year in hopes of saving their homes, they do so without all the facts from the bank. A recent research paper by *Professor Katherine Porter reveals that frequently, banks do not provide homeowners an accurate statement of their accounts before (or after) the debtors are forced into bankruptcy.

The problem with this is, if a homeowner does not know how much is owed on their mortgage then they are making life-changing decisions without the most important facts. As Professor Porter points out, a homeowner may have made a different choice had they known the true amount of the debt. Debtors may have borrowed from family, friends or another source to get the account up-to-date instead of going through court.

Often banks do not comply with requests for an accurate statement of an account. If you make a written request for a statement, they must reply.

Be sure to send the letter to your bank via certified mail. If the bank does not comply, file a complaint with your state attorney general and request they get the info for you.

In my own situation, even after I received a statement of my account no one could understand how much was owed and for what. This problem infests both civil and bankruptcy courts as servicing companies offer very few examples of good, or accurate, accounting. Even after the legal process of discovery and a resulting jury trial, I still have not seen an accurate statement of my account. The same may be true for you.

*_Misbehavior and Mistake in Bankruptcy Mortgage Claims_ by Katherine Porter, Associate Professor University of Iowa College of Law, BA, Yale University, cum laude, 1996, JD, Harvard Law School, magna cum laude, 2001

FDIC Myths and Reality: How Safe is Your Money

As a part of the Emergency Economic Stabilization Act of 2008. FDIC coverage limits have been increased from $100,000 to $250,000 through December 31, 2009.

Myth 1: All banks are FDIC insured.

Fact: Not true, all banks do not have the protection of the FDIC. Visit: www.fdic.gov/ and use the FDIC's Bank Find to be sure your bank is in deed insured by the federal government.

Myth 2: If a bank fails, the FDIC could take up to 99 years to pay depositors for their insured accounts.

Fact: Federal law requires the FDIC to pay the insured deposits "as soon as possible." Payments are usually made within a few days.

Myth 3: The FDIC only pays failed-bank depositors a percentage of their insured funds.

Fact: Federal law requires the FDIC to pay 100% up to federal the limit, including principal and interest.

Myth 4: The most a consumer can have insured is $100,000.

Fact: Single accounts are insured up to $100,000 and in a joint account your portion is insured up to $100,000. If you are beneficiary of a "revocable trust account" and certain conditions are met you are insured up to $100,000. Remember, FDIC coverage limits have been increased from $100,000 to $250,000 through December 31, 2009.

Myth 5: Changing the order of names or Social Security Numbers can increase the coverage for joint accounts.

Fact: Simply not true. Furthermore, substituting "and" for "or" in account titles, will not increase the insurance coverage.

Myth 6: Any product sold by a bank is insured by the FDIC.

Fact: The FDIC insures deposits, such as checking accounts and certificates of deposit (CDs). Banks offer an array of products: mutual funds, stocks, bonds, annuities, and other insurance products that are not FDIC insured.

Myth 7: Deposits in different branches of the same bank are separately insured.

Fact: It depends how much money is in each account category at the same insured institution: single, joint, retirement, etc. It doesn't matter if the accounts were opened at different branches — the FDIC classifies them as the same bank.

Myth 8: Credit Unions are not insured.

Fact: The FDIC does not insure credit unions. The National Credit Union Administration (NCUA) that is the credit union equivalent of FDIC federally insures credit unions. Individual accounts are insured for $250,000 just the same as the FDIC. This change in insurance is in effect until the end of December 2009 for both banks and credit unions. Check with the National Credit Union Administration at: www.ncua.gov to determine if your credit union is a member of NCUA.

Myth 9: The FDIC keeps track of how much money I have in each account in every bank in the U.S.

Fact: The FDIC does not track this information and states on their site that they have no such knowledge.

Myth 10: The FDIC is broke.

Fact: Although the Federal Deposit Insurance Corp. Chairman Sheila Bair stated in a letter, of March 2, 2009, to bankers nationwide regarding increases in FDIC fees "Without these assessments, the deposit insurance fund could become insolvent this year," many "experts" say the program will survive.

The prevailing thought on this is, it is too big to fail and therefore will be funded by an increase in fees and an additional bailout. The FDIC is seeking to have its fund raised from 30 billion to 500 billion.

Nothing is impossible, just improbable, and we are certainly living in extraordinary times. What the "experts" don't know or want to admit is that we may be entering a depression that could last for a decade or more and it is anyone's guess what the world will look like after all of the carnage.

The real pessimists like myself believe the only thing left standing will be the FDIC and McDonalds and some of us have their wager only on McDonalds. Let's not rush to panic; there will be plenty of time for that later. Would you like an apple pie with that?

Fighting The Zombie Banks

There has been much carnage in the banking world as one financial entity after another has given up the ghost and many more promise to follow. Bad events continue to unfold at an ever increasing and malicious rate.

Customer service and client satisfaction has never been a strong point with the mortgage-banking crowd. Accurate bookkeeping, transparent deals and brutal delinquent fees, accompanied by abusive collections practice have been business as usual. Many "experts" insist, in the face of the current economic crisis, banks will have to reform their sinful ways. Don't bet on it.

"Zombie Bank" is a term used to define the fiscally dead and morally bankrupt financial institutions that are standing only because the government props them up. There are a number of dead banks that haven't yet picked the pockets of Uncle Sam.

These banks have had massive lay-offs, their offices are empty, the phones ring, the lights are on, but nobody is in. The remnants of your bank may only be a few employees doling out abusive and physically improbable suggestions when servicing your loan. In the dark, damp, dire bowels of your bank's subbasement resides the rat-fed legal team that will manufacture nightmares sure to keep you and your babies awake for years.

The "experts" on all the cable-news channels assure us homeowners that our banks will be more inclined to work with us so that we can pay our mortgages in these scary financial times. Your experience will probably be more like my own and the millions of others that fell behind on their loan payments.

Does it seem like the more questions or problems you have with your loan, the more you are passed in rapid succession from one callus customer service zombie to the next? As your payments become later, does your bank offer cruel and impossible payment plans as a curative? Are you getting conflicting data on how much you actually owe? These are just a few symptoms that your bank is dead from the neck up. As the death spreads, they devour their customers.

Don't be surprised if your mortgage banker is dragging their butts a bit more than normal. These people are experiencing massive job loss, they are now worried about their own rear-ends and office efficiency is no one's priority. The folks at the bank are freaking-out and they really don't care about you.

If your bank is doing any of these things, I suggest you take the initiative and strike first. Ask for a statement of your account, in writing, and see how the zombies respond. Many homeowners are astonished to find such basic requests denied and they must pursue the matter with their state attorney general.

The simple action of requesting a statement of your account and being denied is a violation of federal law, the Truth in Lending Laws (TILA) to be exact. Chances are if there is one violation in the woodpile there are more. This is the point where I sought legal counsel and filed a lawsuit against my zombie bank.

Have a Plan: Foreclosure And Your Pets

There are many victims in the tsunami of foreclosures sweeping the nation. Among the most vulnerable in these uncertain times are the pets that have become family. It is unfortunate that as families are uprooted and forced from their homes into rentals or even homelessness, their pets are left behind. The practice is so common that "foreclosure pets" has become the term to describe the unfortunate occurrence.

Before you abandon your pet to the elements and hazards of living on the street or endanger your animal by placing them in a temporary situation that is not suitable, think about what you are doing. Consider what is best for your pet and determine what solution is safest for all.

Many well meaning animal lovers make mistakes when they try to find short-term living conditions for their pets while they complete a move. Be very careful. Aunt Kate may be your favorite family member but incapable of caring for your dog or cat.

Penning your animal up at a friend's house may have been a good intentioned plan poorly thought out. Your dog or cat will probably be anxious and inclined to make a run for it. Well meaning plans can easily put your animal friend in danger. It is all too common that one way or another pets end up on the street.

In warmer climates, such as Florida, there have been notable sightings of exotic pets such as nonnative birds, large snakes and other reptiles let loose by owners as they decide they cannot afford to keep the animal and move on, abandoning their pets.

Releasing your animals onto the streets to fend for themselves in the urban or suburban setting is a level of dumb and cruel that I hope catches up with people who do this. Taking the family pet on "a long ride" out into farm country is also poor judgment; many ill-fated pets don't last long out there.

Abandoning your pet is a criminal offense in every state. Regardless of the sort of pet you have, don't leave them behind. Contact your local animal shelters for assistance and ask them about the services they provide and how the process works, take an interest in how your pet will be cared for and what will ultimately be done with them.

If local resources are strained, do not exist or you are attempting to locate a home or foster care for either a specific breed of dog or cat, a ferret, reptile or exotic birds, do an internet search. Include the specific type of animal and the state you live in, there are rescues for every kind of animal you can imagine.

For additional information to assist you in finding a new home or temporary foster care contact the following organizations:

No Paws Left Behind, Inc.
Is a 501c3 non-profit organization dedicated to bringing awareness to and finding solutions for the growing phenomena of "foreclosure pets" by directing visitors, based on their zip code, to local animal shelters and other alternative housing providers for pets in need
www.NoPawsLeftBehind.org

The Humane Society of the United States
Has a link to local shelters and other information

Half Of Banks Can't Prove They Own Mortgages

You would probably think it insane if I were to tell you that your bank might not have any legal right to collect on your mortgage or threaten foreclosure. The truth is, the chances of your bank being unable to prove your debt is more in your favor than you would ever believe.

A recent research paper published in the Texas Law Review* provides some disturbing facts regarding bad banking practices. A study of 1,700 bankruptcy cases proved; banks cannot produce the note 41% of the time and they cannot produce a security instrument 19% of the time. The results further indicate that one or more pieces of required documentation is missing 52% of the time.

When threatened with foreclosure, millions of people have abandoned their homes and have done so largely without a fight. Had they only known that a "technicality" could have voided or renegotiated their loans; they may not have left their homes so easily or agreed to the claims against them in bankruptcy court.

Simply put, your bank is required by law to have the proper paperwork to prove how much you owe, who has the legal right to collect the debt, and if the debt is securitized by a deed of trust or other lien on your property.

What does all this mean to people having trouble with their bank, filing bankruptcy, or facing foreclosure? If the bank does not have a legal lien on your property then it is not a mortgage loan, it is a personal debt and they cannot take your property by foreclosure. If the bank does not have the note, there is no accurate way to determine how much you owe and if they are the entity legally entitled to collect the debt.

Unfortunately many attorneys and judges do not know, or follow, the consumer credit laws and many claims against the consumer go uncontested. Don't let this happen to you, demand the proof from the bank that they have the legal right to collect the debt.

*_Misbehavior and Mistake in Bankruptcy Mortgage Claims_ by Katherine Porter, Associate Professor University of Iowa College of Law,

BA, Yale University, cum laude, 1996, JD, Harvard Law School, magna cum laude, 2001

How the Courts Fail You Everyday

The biggest mistake homeowner's make is abandoning their homes without a fight. There is plenty of bad advice from "experts" telling people to cut their losses, send the keys to the bank, and just go on with your life. Abandoning your home should be your last option. The important thing to know is that you do have an array of consumer rights both state and federal and I am willing to wager your bank is abusing some of them. This alone does not make your task easy or a sure thing.

There may be a number of ways to determine if you are dealing with a bad home loan that may contain fraud. For example: the loan you have is not what you thought you where getting (bait and switch), there was an inflated appraisal, your mortgage broker lied. On the servicing end you may have a bank returning mortgage payments, using foul and threatening language, charging you arbitrary fines and fees or refusing to give you an accurate statement of your account. All of these actions break the law.

The challenges a consumer confronts going up against credit card companies, mortgage bankers and other creditors in either bankruptcy or civil courts may leave you the worse for wear and wondering what exactly went wrong. For starters it is tough to find lawyers that specialize in consumer law, let alone something as specialized as predatory lending. Another challenge is finding a law firm that is not a legal "mill" which handles hundreds of cases a year with poor representation.

A recent academic study reveals bankruptcy courts, their judges, and lawyers representing the consumer or debtor overwhelmingly fail the nation on a daily basis. The result is millions of consumers are in danger of being underrepresented or misrepresented and therefore paying a debt to a creditor that does not have legal claim to such collections.

A horrific revelation in Professor Porter's paper, *"Misbehavior and Mistake in Bankruptcy Mortgage Claims"* recently published in the Texas Law Review is that a lot of homeowners are getting screwed in the process of filing Chapter 13 bankruptcy. The failure is systemic and runs rotten throughout the nation's bankruptcy courts at the expense and peril of the consumer.

Professor Porter's findings show that 96% of consumers never object to the amount the creditors say they owe even though the creditor and consumer agree on how much was owed only 4.4% of the time. This leaves a whopping 95.6% of the time when bank and the homeowner did not agree on the amount of a mortgage debt.

It is all the more vexing when you consider other important numbers from *Misbehavior and Mistake in Bankruptcy Mortgage Claims*. Banks cannot produce the note 41% of the time and they cannot produce a security instrument 19% of the time. The results further indicate that one or more pieces of required documentation is missing 52% of the time.

This is a failure of attorneys representing consumers and judges not requiring all the documentation. The current system is flawed as countless Americans are rushed through a process without the benefit of having their rights upheld. Bankruptcy court is not the only place people don't do their jobs.

Consumer issues that require a civil remedy, such as suing a predatory lender or an abusive mortgage servicer, almost always resolve themselves through mediation and do not go to court. This is of course if you and your bank can come to some kind of terms for a settlement. The fact is there is a culture of settling in the legal world which breeds lazy lawyers who may not prepare enough for court.

My own experience with hiring a legal weasel was as unpleasant and as disappointing as it could have been. After six years of under-performance, disinterest and downright legal malpractice the only thing worse would have been not having an attorney.

The best way to be certain you are being properly represented, under either civil law or federal bankruptcy law, is to be vigilant throughout the process. Be interested in what is happening and take notes. Ask questions of your lawyer and be sure you get answers.

*_Misbehavior and Mistake in Bankruptcy Mortgage Claims_ by Katherine Porter, Associate Professor University of Iowa College of Law, BA, Yale University, cum laude, 1996, JD, Harvard Law School, magna cum laude, 2001

How To Hire A Lawyer To Save Your Home

So, you are having trouble with your mortgage company and most experts are advising homeowners turn their key over to the banks and rent. You don't see an alternative to foreclosure and leaving your home; not so fast. You have rights and you need to "exercise" them.

Making written requests for 1) the note, 2) security instrument and 3) an itemized statement of your account can send your bank into a paralysis trying to produce documents they must legally provide. Many times the lender cannot provide a security instrument and are at a loss to force a foreclosure.

Requesting these documents can easily progress to you having to retain an attorney to file a civil suit because they don't provide them. You may be a victim of predatory lending in that you received a high fee, high interest loan. You may have got a loan different than the one you were promised, you may have been subject to abusive collection practices; all reasons to sue your bank.

You need to contact legal aid in your area to see if you qualify for their services. Other options include legal assistance from local college or university law school programs and pro bono legal programs.

The steps described below usually take years to complete. In my own situation it took six years before it reached court.

- Once you have a lawyer the lender is no longer allowed to have any contact with you directly. All correspondence must be through your attorney.

- All collection actions are put on hold.

- Any violations are included in a proper complaint. This formal complaint is filed with a circuit or federal court and pursued as a civil suit.

- Once the complaint is filed in a court, the bad bankers will have approximately 30 days to respond.

- ? The first response by the offending lender is to deny any wrongdoing and to "paper" your attorney. This refers to a common process by which the defendant's legal team responds to the plaintiff's lawyer with a pile of papers. There will be several pages of answers to the allegations and several more pages of requests for statements of the facts and documentation of the wrongdoing. The documents collected will fill several boxes before it is over.

- ? All sides named in your lawsuit will give depositions. A deposition is testimony (outside of the courtroom) given under oath, detailing what has happened. You have not lived until you have been deposed by corporate lawyers asking you questions for four or five hours. It is like pulling teeth without the benefit of anesthesia, as legal weasels turn the question and answer phase into something medieval. Brace yourself for this, it can be punishing. Just remember these attorneys want to intimidate you; stick to your guns tell the truth and just let them know at every turn you expect to leave the case for a jury of your peers to decide and not you or anyone other than a jury, as a matter of being unbiased and fair.

? Your lawyer should make requests for 1) the note, 2) security instrument, 3) an itemized statement of your account and any other documents they have concerning your loan. This can send your bank into a paralysis trying to produce documents they must legally provide. Many times the lender cannot provide a security instrument and are at a loss to force a foreclosure.

? Most states would rather both parties reach an agreement by means of arbitration or negotiation. If all else fails, you have the right to appear in court and have a jury decide. You also have the right to not mediate at all, and insist upon a jury trial.

The majority of predatory loan situations reaching this point end in a settlement instead of a trial. This is determined by how willing your bank is to workout an amiable deal and how effective your attorney is in negotiating.

You can expect frustration with the amount time the process takes, the asinine things your bank will try and even the performance of your own lawyer. The end of the ordeal will leave you tired and beaten up; there will be no thought of victory, only one of survival.

For legal aid information in your area visit **www.consumershock.org** and click on resources.

How To Stop Foreclosure

The first thing a homeowner needs to do is keep communicating with the bank. Don't wait until you fall behind to see if you qualify for a temporary payment plan or a complete modification of your loan. Try to work out some kind of deal; this is good advice when your bank is willing to work with you. It is far more likely your bank will abuse you, given the opportunity, and will crush you and your family.

I have personally deployed all of the following methods in defense of my home. These techniques worked for me and they will work for you. To make any of this advice work you must be relentless in taking the steps to stop the bank from foreclosing. This may only provide you with a delay and give you some valuable time to save money to move into a rental.

When in imminent threat of being tossed out, filing bankruptcy or a civil suit will grant you an automatic stay, or legal pause, on the foreclosure process. With the new bankruptcy laws in effect, a judge can reduce your mortgage and alter the terms. I recommend that you make appointments with a number of lawyers seeking free advice regarding your particular situation. The first visit is always free.

While you are looking for lawyers contact your local legal aid office and see if you qualify for their free legal services. If so, get signed up. You should also contact a HUD-Approved Housing Counselor to determine what options are avaible to you.

You will be visiting several offices, be sure to take all your paperwork, this includes copies of all records regarding your loan including those from the courthouse. You also need to find out what the accepted security instrument is in your state, the deed of trust or the mortgage note and the rules of document recording. Be sure to request from your bank a certified copy of the original mortgage note and proof the bank has a legal security instrument, as required by your state's laws, or in other words, an enforceable lien on your home.

Making written requests for 1) the note, 2) the security instrument and 3) an itemized statement of your account can send your bank into a paralysis trying to produce documents they must legally provide. Many times the lender cannot provide a security instrument and does not have the legal right to force a foreclosure.

There is a multitude of documents I recommend you request from your bank:

1. The note
2. Security instrument
3. An itemized statement of your account
4. Itemized statement of escrow account separate from the loan account
5. Copy of loan pool and servicing agreement stating who is the servicer of the loan and who owns note They are usually two different companies.
6. Complete transaction history of your loan
7. Indemnification agreement between servicer and the owner of your mortgage note

If you already know they can't provide 1 and/or 2 file a request for release of the lien and mortgage.

Many of these documents are never provided, even during the discovery process, so don't be surprised if they will not give them up without filing a lawsuit. The main point here is you need to stay ahead of the bank by making them prove they have legal right to collect the debt or foreclose.

I would be far more surprised that a loan, after professional scrutiny, did not contain some element that could void the mortgage or force a renegotiation of terms. The mortgage banking system is really this fouled up and you need to know this before you abandon your home.

Contact HUD (800) 569-4287 by phone or search by state for a a HUD-Approved Housing Counselor
http://www.hud.gov/offices/hsg/sfh/hcc/hcs.cfm

Mortgage Nightmares to Learn From

The nightmare is that ten thousand families are losing their homes to foreclosure everyday. The crisis is spreading through America like a wildfire leaving neighborhoods devastated, devalued and empty. Many families will never recover from this disaster and such a massive displacement will have repercussions for generations.

"Experts" giving bad advice on all the cable news channels and elsewhere exacerbate the problem. I am not saying there is no useful information; the problem is the people giving the advice are often people making six figures or more a year and they have no real firsthand experience. When fighting foreclosure or war you better take someone's advice that has direct knowledge through doing. It is the difference between kicking ass or having yours kicked.

The first mistake people make is just giving up and walking away. The reason most homeowners do this is because they will not or cannot work a deal with the bank. Some of the prevalent bad advice going around is directing homeowners to just rollover and send the keys to the bank.

When the bank has you up against the wall with a loan you cannot afford, you can use a short or long-term strategy. If they are going to foreclose it could take 60 days, 90 days or more, this could buy you enough time to save money, make arrangements and move to a rental. A long-term strategy is to file a civil suit if you believe something is wrong with your mortgage. Filing a lawsuit may suspend your payments and can put you in a good position to negotiate a settlement or loan modification.

The very fact you have a loan you cannot afford or more precisely have not been able to afford since the beginning of the loan, is revealing. There is a debt-to-income-ratio formula lenders must follow when underwriting a loan and you not being able to pay your mortgage may indicate foul play.

Ask yourself honestly, did you get the loan you expected? Was your interest rate higher than you were promised? Did the broker sneak in an adjustable rate mortgage or a balloon loan you did not understand or know about? If so, these are all grounds to consider legal action.

Consider any other nightmarish experiences you may have had with your loan. In retrospect does anything seem weird or just not right? Was your loan closed at a fast-food restaurant or other "odd" place? How about the company taking your payments, have they been keeping an accurate account for you, are you being overcharged, have they been rude or failed to comply with requests regarding your loan?

There is no "magic bullet" for families that can guarantee they will keep their homes using the legal system. However, by not using the legal system, you will surely lose your home.

In the event things go from bad to worse, as they so often do, remember that you have rights. Consult an attorney, as well as, a certified HUD counselor for advice.

More Mortgage Nightmares to Learn From

The nightmarish aspects of your home loan may appear shortly after closing or they may take months or even years to make themselves known. Most homeowners never see the monster lurking within their mortgage until it has them by the throat. Here are some common examples of mortgage nightmares you may be having.

The Andersons decided to refinance their mortgage while interest rates were low; wanting to lock in a better rate with a thirty-year fixed rate. The loan they ended up with was not a fixed rate mortgage but an adjustable one. What was believed to be a 30-year mortgage, turned out to be a 15-year balloon loan. They later found the loan originator, the loan broker and the closing agent had overcharged them.

The Johnson family refinanced their mortgage getting cash out to add a bedroom and replace the roof. The monthly payments they had to pay exceeded the amount agreed to at closing by $200.00 and no one at their bank had any answers. When the family fell behind on payments the bank demanded a large sum of cash to cover the alleged late fees. Soon thereafter, the bank began to demand more cash or they would foreclose.

The Gonzales ran into trouble with the bank's accounting inaccuracies which only snowballed becoming more problematic. Even after paying several large payments to their account, late fees continued to pile up. All the while the bank refused to comply with repeated requests for an itemized statement of their account. Soon after, the family was contacted by the bank's lawyers with a letter to cure default, if not properly handled foreclosure would be coming soon.

The Jones family had been paying their mortgage on time for two years. Then one day a bank they never heard of before contacted them and started threatening foreclosure. If they did not pay thousands of dollars soon they would lose their home within a few months. It seemed unreal that an unknown bank would appear out of nowhere while you were still paying another bank.

First and foremost remember you have rights and banks would like you to believe you don't. The biggest mistake people make is abandoning their homes when they don't have to legally do so. Of course, communicate with your lender to work things out; but be prepared for the bank to be unreasonable and unwilling to negotiate a payment plan you can live with.

In the event things go from bad to worse, as they so often do, remember that you have rights. Consult with an attorney as well as a certified HUD counselor for advice.

Ninety Percent Of Borrowers Are Unhappy With Their Mortgage Servicer

According to a study by *Professor Katherine Porter, ninety percent of people with mortgages are unhappy with their servicers. The number indicates many people are having some bad loan experiences. Your bad experiences may violate consumer laws and be grounds for suing your bank. This could result in the loan being voided or the terms being renegotiated in your favor.

Bad business is standard operating procedure for banks, and homeowners don't like it. Most people are so desensitized to the pushy, uncompromising attitudes and the poor accounting habits of their bank, that they give little thought to the overall bad behavior in regards to their consumer rights. Our banks are rude, obnoxious, and deceptive, but are they doing anything wrong or illegal?

What your bank does not want you to know is that you have rights under state and federal law. If the company servicing your mortgage is being abusive or threatening, then you may have grounds to sue. If your account balance is not accurate or the bank refuses to provide you with an accurate written statement of your account, then you need to see a lawyer.

The Federal Trade Commission has identified several illegal charges routinely added to loan accounts by banks, for example, unwarranted late fees, unnecessary insurance, warehouse fees, and other miscellaneous fees. These particular abuses go largely undetected by a homeowner until it is too late. Identifying these violations requires an expert in state and federal law, as well as, forensic accounting skills.

Servicing agents are bad people that use strong-arm tactics in collection; they are negligent and deceptive in billing, accounting and noncompliance to requests. This is why almost every American dislikes their servicing agent and why many people seek an attorney to stop these abusive collection and predatory lending practices. Remember, nothing stops foreclosure like filing a civil suit.

Misbehavior and Mistake in Bankruptcy Mortgage Claims by Katherine Porter, Associate Professor University of Iowa College of Law,

BA, Yale University, cum laude, 1996, JD, Harvard Law School, magna cum laude, 2001

Sins Of The Mortgage Servicer

All too often when the subject of predatory lending comes up the focus is on the front end of the deal or at origination and funding. The attention is on fraudulent documentation, inflated appraisals, falsification by broker of debt-to-income-ratio of applicant and other shady elements that occurred at the beginning of your loan.

The biggest unexplored continent of bad banking is the abuses of the banking institutions collecting monthly payments. This dark, doomed and vast wasteland soon to be discovered is where the real horrors of the insanity of abusive, terroristic and incompetent banking reside. It is a mad reality where lenders use mafia-like collection tactics on loans they may have no legal right to.

More often than not thugs at the bank using abusive and deceptive collection methods overwhelm a homeowner. The large number of people leaving their homes demonstrates that when things go bad between the mortgage servicer and the homeowner the latter loses their home and almost always without a fight.

It all starts with problems regarding making payments or an inaccuracy or disagreement with billing. I have found many people have been victimized by banks extorting amounts of money out of homeowners all the while charging additional late fees and even skewing the amount owed on the mortgage.

Usually, things continue to deteriorate between homeowner and banker until families feel they have no other choice than to give up the keys and walk away from their homes. Unfortunately, people take bad advice by "experts" telling people to just abandon their houses without even considering their rights.

I cannot be more opposed to those that recommend the "roll over doctrine" and tell folks to give up the idea of homeownership and rent. I am an advocate of the "school of unrelenting attacks if you screw with me." I suggest you too become a follower of "the way" and to do so you must first replace the fear your mortgage company has cultivated in you with a healthy crop of anger.

Your mortgage servicer wants you to believe you have no rights and that you must do whatever they say, not so fast. Generally, I have found mortgage bankers to be the worst violators of consumer rights around; there is not even a close second. With this in mind take that healthy and polite harvest of anger and start asking questions about your loan. Your bank has to provide account information. Make your bank prove they have the details of your loan right; it is your legal right to do so.

Making written requests for 1) the note, 2) the security instrument and 3) an itemized statement of your account can send your bank into a paralysis trying to produce documents they must legally provide. Many times the lender cannot provide a security instrument and are at a loss to force a foreclosure.

When You Can't Trust Bankers

A lot of folks are anxious over the recent economic downturn and daily news descriptions including the mantra " since The Great Depression" have many wondering what happened and how we have reached the edge and perhaps soon the abyss. The crisis we are in now is the result of a lack of confidence caused by some really shady business dealings.

The entire mess began with home loans. These mortgages were not your grandparents' mortgages; in fact, these loans could not be further from those time-tested and stable transactions. In "the old days" when you went to the bank for a loan it was a local bank that loaned you the money and held your loan. This same bank would have collected the payments on your loan until your mortgage was paid off. The business deal was very basic and straightforward, not like the banking system we have today.

Bankers have lobbied congress until they got their wish list turned to law. What the law made possible was a financial shell game. A typical loan goes through many hands on the way to the final servicer. The loan may have passed through five entities before you even make your first payment. Your loan has been originated, brokered, warehoused, underwritten, and assigned to a servicer. The process has been made complicated and deceptive on purpose.

Bad banking policies and low-interest teaser rates lured many people into loans they could not afford. Within the banking system, a lot more was going on than lax regulations and well-marketed deals. There was also an abundance of fraud going on; inflated appraisals, document tampering and other predatory lending practices. Many homeowners were ripped off by "bait and switch" loan offers; the loans they were promised is not the loan they got.

The problem is further complicated when some Wall Street wizards thought it a good idea to "pool" or bring these loans together into a collective. These loan "pools" or mortgage-backed securities (MBS) were bought by investors and became part of investment and retirement plans.

There was a lot riding on these loans: homes, investment portfolios, and the credibility of the lending institutions. Once people started defaulting on loans they could not afford and were foreclosed on, this foreclosure depressed the prices of homes in their neighborhood. As foreclosures increase, property prices plunge drastically causing many mortgages to "underwater" meaning that the homeowner's mortgage debt is higher than the property value. This has resulted in more and more people abandoning their homes.

The total devastation that is sweeping through the housing market has exposed the mortgage-backed security (MBS) investments for what they are: a scam. Unfortunately, the damage will be far and wide destroying the retirement plans many have been building for a lifetime.

There is no trust among the banks because they really do not know how much bad debt they or their associates have within their institutions. This lack of trust has cut off lending to everyone, you, me, businesses, and other banks. This complete shutdown of liquidity or cash has frozen the economy. Consequently, the economy is shrinking meaning that we are in a recession and perhaps a severe and long sustained recession or depression is in our future if the cycle of destruction continues unchecked. Bad things happen when you can't trust bankers.

Who Really Owns Your Home?

As the banking system slips beneath the waves pulling millions of us along, people are overwhelmed with fear and disbelief. The cable news "experts" have no real idea how big the monsters are, and the bankers that created this unholy mess will rain down from skyscrapers before they will tell where all the bodies are buried.

We all know that it was bad business practices on the part of bankers that have brought us perhaps the next depression. What many folks don't know is that the banker's business deals were much more rotten than one could have ever imagined. So much so, that there is a good chance the bank can't provide an original mortgage note or a legal security instrument.

Everyone reading this needs to request information regarding the whereabouts of the original note or mortgage for their loan. The next thing you need to do is visit the records office at your local courthouse to see if all of the documents regarding your loan have been recorded. This includes all the assignments of the security instrument. The latter may not be so obvious and may require a title search by an attorney.

It may seem unbelievable that banking is so screwed up that lenders may have lost required documentation proving they have a mortgage or any right to collect on a loan. It is a common occurrence that is getting more media coverage to the dismay of banks everywhere.

In my own situation I had a bank trying to foreclose on me that had no enforceable security instrument and they no longer owned my loan. They had sold my loan years earlier; this did not stop them from appearing in court and misrepresenting their interests/stake in my loan and stating under oath they owned/had rights to my mortgage.

A grandmother in Georgia has been fighting a bad bank for a number of years. After making payments on time for years she had been contacted by the bank that informed her none of the payments had been received/recorded.

A women living in Florida had all of her belongings thrown out. While dealing with one bank another lender, she never heard of, began foreclosure proceedings.

Returning to my own bad loan as an example, even though there is a lot of documentation regarding the security instrument, none of them were recorded. In my state it is essential that the assignments of a deed be recorded in the correct order of transfer from one institution to the next. The bank's title search on my property revealed they did not have an enforceable lien and could not foreclose.

Oh sure, the fraudsters provided a lot of paperwork surrounding my deed. I have seven assignments or transfers of my deed none of them are worth the paper they are forged on. There are many things wrong with these notarized documents including possible notary fraud but what is most important is in a state of record they did not follow the law and record their rights to my loan in the correct order. There was more wrong with my predatory mortgage but that was enough to void the loan.

Contact HUD (800) 569-4287 by phone or search by state for a a HUD-Approved Housing Counselor
http://www.hud.gov/offices/hsg/sfh/hcc/hcs.cfm

Question 1

Question: What is the difference between Chapter 7 and Chapter 13 bankruptcy and which is best for me?

Answer: Chapter 7 bankruptcy is a liquidation or sale of a debtor's nonexempt property after which proceeds are paid to creditors. There is no payment plan setup as in Chapter 13 instead a trustee gathers and sells your assets to pay the creditors that have filed a claim against you.

Chapter 13 bankruptcy also known as Individual Debt Adjustment is a process whereby a consumer may save his or her property. The protections under this chapter of bankruptcy make it possible for a debtor, with a steady income, to enter a payment plan and pay creditors an agreed upon amount.

As a result of changes in bankruptcy laws in 2005, you must file a certificate of credit counseling from a U.S. Trustee-approved credit counselor and a copy of any debt repayment plan.

The Chapter 13 process can take three years to five years to complete an agreed upon payment plan, which is monitored by a bankruptcy trustee. The Chapter 7 bankruptcy is usually completed in a few months as a trustee gathers and sells your assets. Another difference between the two filings is Chapter 13 will usually appear on your credit record for seven years whereas Chapter 7 will be on your credit record for ten years even though the Fair Credit Reporting Act allows all bankruptcies to stay on your report for 10 years.

Chapter 13 has a particular advantage because it provides homeowners with an opportunity to save their homes from foreclosure by allowing them to "catch up" past due payments through a payment plan. In Chapter 7 part of the debtor's property may be subject to liens and mortgages that pledge the property to other creditors.

New rules that went into effect in 2009 will allow bankruptcy judges to modify a mortgage. Previous to this, judges were unable to modify a mortgage but could void it if it did not meet certain requirements.

Chapter 13 also requires specific documentation that should be requested by your attorney and this can have dire consequences for creditors who don't play by the rules. A recent study by Prof. Porter revealed a disturbing number of the mortgages reviewed were missing one or more of three required pieces of documentation.

Allow me to explain, when you file bankruptcy your creditors must file what is known as "proofs" or claims in order to collect on the debt they say you owe. Bankruptcy law requires that mortgage companies provide three documents, a "perfected" instrument of security, the note, and an accurate itemized statement of your account. Banks are notorious for not producing all three required documents.

Unfortunately few claims are ever challenged and more distressing yet, the trio of required documents are not requested by a debtor's attorney and a mortgage that may have been cancelled by a bankruptcy judge is left standing. Recently some bankruptcy judges have been throwing out claims by mortgage companies incapable of providing the three required documents. An absence of such documentation should spark many questions and may make a homeowner reconsider filing bankruptcy in favor of a civil suit.

What is best for you will be determined by whether you have steady income, live in a home that you are trying to save and qualify for a payment schedule; this would be Chapter 13. If you do not have an income and cannot enter a repayment plan, Chapter 7 is the alternative.

As of 2005 filing bankruptcy has become more difficult. If you qualify, recent changes as of 2009 may make bankruptcy a practical solution for you. The complexities and requirements of bankruptcy filings require you consult a lawyer that specializes in bankruptcy law.

Question 2

Question: How does the Chapter 13 process work?

Answer: The Chapter 13 bankruptcy procedure begins with you filing a petition with the bankruptcy court that has jurisdiction where you reside. There is a $235 case filing fee and a $39 miscellaneous administrative fee. The court will require: 1) an accounting of all your assets and liabilities; 2) income and expenses; 3) a list of contracts and leases; and; 4) a statement of your financial affairs 5) As a result of changes in bankruptcy laws in 2005, you must also file a certificate of credit counseling and a copy of any debt repayment plan developed through a U.S. Trustee-approved credit counselor.

You will need a statement of your income earned within the last sixty-days, a list of current expenses and state whether you anticipate any future increase in either income or expenses; you will of course need your tax returns for the most recent tax year as well as returns filed during the case.

You will be required to submit a repayment plan with your petition or no later than fifteen-days, unless the court grants you an extension on filing. Your repayment plan must be submitted to and approved by the court. You will have to be able to pay a bankruptcy trustee regular payments (bi-weekly or monthly) who then pays your creditors according to the agreed upon plan.

A debtor usually appears in court for two hearings the first involves your creditors and the second is a confirmation of your payment plan. More hearings may be required if complications arise. The first hearing is usually held about a month after the case is filed the second, your confirmation hearing, may be held on the same day but no later than 45 days after.

Within thirty days after filing the bankruptcy case, even if the court has not approved the plan, you must start making payments to the trustee. If the court does not confirm your plan (or a modification) and dismisses the case you may not get all of your money back. You could be charged court costs and any funds already disbursed to your creditors will not be returned.

The trustee must return any remaining funds to you.

If your plan is confirmed and you make scheduled payments that meet your obligation, your bankruptcy will be discharged. A discharge is a court order releasing you from all applicable debt. There are two types of Chapter 13 discharges a full, or successfully completed one, and a partial or unsuccessful discharge. The later discharge is court ordered in particular circumstances if a debtor is not capable of completing the payment plan.

If during the payment schedule you are unable to make payments as a result of losing your job or some other reason, the court may modify or suspend your payment plan until you can afford to pay.

In any event, if the debtor fails to make the payments due under the confirmed plan, the court may dismiss the case or convert it to a liquidation case under Chapter 7 of the Bankruptcy Code.

Question 3

Question: What has changed so drastically with the bankruptcy laws and is it even possible to file?

Answer: Prior to the changes made in 2005 it was easy to file and to be able to "write-off" or dismiss your debt entirely. Now there are standards or qualifiers that potential applicants must have and you will have to repay some debt through liquidation of your belongings or entering into a repayment plan.

Question: How do I know if Chapter 13 bankruptcy is a solution for me and can I protect my home?

Answer: For one thing you need to have an income. This particular kind of filing can protect your home by allowing you to pay your delinquent payments. Recent changes to bankruptcy laws allow judges to "cram down" or readjust the stated value of your home when you owe more than your home is worth. Judges are now able to modify the terms of a mortgage to help families keep their homes.

A recent research paper* published in the Texas Law Review provides some disturbing facts regarding bad banking practices in 1,700 Chapter 13 bankruptcy cases. The truth is, banks cannot produce the note 41% of the time and they cannot produce a security instrument 19% of the time.

Furthermore, your bank must file a claim against you and notify the court as to how much you owe them and why. The same study has shown that there is a frequent discrepancy between the homeowner and the bank as to how much is owed. Unfortunately, claims are hardly ever reviewed or contested by the consumer or their legal representation.

I encourage everyone considering Chapter 13 to visit www.consumershock.org and read Misbehavior and Mistake in Bankruptcy Mortgage Claims by Katherine Porter, Associate Professor University of Iowa College of Law, BA, Yale University, cum laude, 1996, JD, Harvard Law School, magna cum laude, 2001

How does a Chapter 13 bankruptcy plan affect a foreclosure?

There is an immediate "stay" or delay in the foreclosure proceedings. Your bank will probably counter with a motion to request the judge dismiss them from any action because you cannot repay under bankruptcy protections or meet the requirements for a payment plan.

Don't despair this is a common ploy used by banks and with amendments to bankruptcy laws empowering judges with the ability to modify home loans it does not have the same effect.

Even more important be sure the court and your attorney serve their purposes and uphold the laws. This means having all required documentation that proves that your bank has a legal right to collect on a mortgage. This would be a note or mortgage, a legal security instrument and an accurate statement of much you owe.

Question 4

Question: Our bank's reply to requests has ranged from no reply to incomplete replies. We are worried about foreclosure as our bank runs out of patience and applies more pressure to collect. We are so far behind that the bank's legal division is calling us on the phone. They assure us everything they do is lawful.

It seems unlikely that our bank will provide any paperwork on your list of documents to request, it seems even more unlikely that this could ever save our home. So, are we missing the point or is there a "magic bullet" to save the day?

Answer: There is oftentimes no easy fix or "magic bullet" to remedy homeowner and banker differences. You are mistaken if you believe your bank does not have to follow federal law regarding account information.

Being contacted by the bank's legal division before you are actually in foreclosure or receive a notice to cure default is not standard operating procedure.

Mortgage company personal handle the collection process throughout the delinquent stages. This includes forbearance; when homeowners are required to enter a special payment schedule that will require one or more lump sums to catch up on payments.

Lawyers do not enter the scene until a homeowner is contacted with the ultimatum to pay the note in full or face foreclosure. It is more likely that your bank has presented their selves as lawyers when they are not; this too is a violation of federal law. It is a common practice for bad bankers to turn up the pressure by using these types of methods.

Something is rotten at your mortgage company; lawyers are not part of the "in-house" collection process. Furthermore, lawyers would not contact you over the phone but only in writing. It strikes me as absurd that real legal representation would "assure us everything they do is legal." It is more likely you are not speaking to a real attorney and are a victim of abusive and illegal collection practices.

In closing I really want to hit home, or homes as it were, what I offer. The truth is, there are no quick fixes when dealing with bad banks. None of the problems I have encountered has ever been resolved without a homeowner standing up for their rights and this means finding your own legal representation to be certain that your bank is not breaking the law.

Don't think I am "lawyer happy," I am not, they are a necessary evil in a nasty world. I am not telling people to "lawyer up" to win a fortune in a settlement or court battle. There is no jackpot at the end of the legal rainbow. What I offer is the knowledge I gained through my experiences during the very long and painful process of saving my home.

You are going into a battle that can take years. I hope to give folks an idea of what to expect and prepare for, as they try to save their homes. I do not offer a quick fix; I recommend you keep reading G. B. Taken throughout your ordeal because I will tell you the facts, as no one else will. You will benefit from what you learn here even after you have a lawyer; my advice will help you make sure you have someone representing you for real, not just going through the motions.

Question 5

Question: I am in big trouble how can I stop foreclosure?

Answer: The first thing a homeowner needs to do is keep communicating with the bank. Don't wait until you fall behind to see if you qualify for a temporary payment plan or a complete modification of your loan. Try to work out some kind of deal; this is good advice when your bank is willing to work with you. It is far more likely your bank will abuse you, given the opportunity, and will crush you and your family.

I have personally deployed all of the following methods in defense of my home. These techniques worked for me and they will work for you. To make any of this advice work you must be relentless in taking the steps to stop the bank from foreclosing. This may only provide you with a delay and give you some valuable time to save money to move into a rental.

When in imminent threat of being tossed out, filing bankruptcy or a civil suit will grant you an automatic stay, or legal pause, on the foreclosure process. With the new bankruptcy laws in effect, a judge can reduce your mortgage and alter the terms. I recommend that you make appointments with a number of lawyers seeking free advice regarding your particular situation. The first visit is always free.

While you are looking for lawyers contact your local legal aid office and see if you qualify for their free legal services. If so, get signed up. You should also contact a HUD-Approved Housing Counselor to determine what options are avaible to you.

You will be visiting several offices, be sure to take all your paperwork, this includes copies of all records regarding your loan including those from the courthouse. You also need to find out what the accepted security instrument is in your state, the deed of trust or the mortgage note and the rules of document recording. Be sure to request from your bank a certified copy of the original mortgage note and proof the bank has a legal security instrument, as required by your state's laws, or in other words, an enforceable lien on your home.

Making written requests for 1) the note, 2) the security instrument and 3) an itemized statement of your account can send your bank into a paralysis trying to produce documents they must legally provide. Many times the lender cannot provide a security instrument and does not have the legal right to force a foreclosure.

There is a multitude of documents I recommend you request from your bank:

1. The note
2. Security instrument
3. An itemized statement of your account
4. Itemized statement of escrow account separate from the loan account
5. Copy of loan pool and servicing agreement stating who is the servicer of the loan and who owns note They are usually two different companies.
6. Complete transaction history of your loan
7. Indemnification agreement between servicer and the owner of your mortgage note

If you already know they can't provide 1 and/or 2 file a request for release of the lien and mortgage.

Many of these documents are never provided, even during the discovery process, so don't be surprised if they will not give them up without filing a lawsuit. The main point here is you need to stay ahead of the bank by making them prove they have legal right to collect the debt or foreclose.

I would be far more surprised that a loan, after professional scrutiny, did not contain some element that could void the mortgage or force a renegotiation of terms. The mortgage banking system is really this fouled up and you need to know this before you abandon your home.

Contact HUD (800) 569-4287 by phone or search by state for a a HUD-Approved Housing Counselor
http://www.hud.gov/offices/hsg/sfh/hcc/hcs.cfm

Question 6

Question: You are always advising homeowners to hire a lawyer. There are companies that prepare documents and show homeowners how to represent themselves in court at a fraction of the cost of an attorney.

I am certain I have a case against my bank but cannot afford an attorney; why not use a service?

Answer: The type of service you are considering has become popular in recent years with the increase of foreclosures. I am suspicious of any company that advises people to represent themselves in court. This is especially true when dealing with the intricacies of state and federal consumer laws and this is only half of the battle.

You have not experienced frustration and agony until you have to deal with the high-powered jackals the bank calls lawyers. Your experiences with your own lawyer will be an ordeal as well. To wade in neck deep without the benefit of your own legal representation puts you in a place you know nothing of and no pseudo-legal entity will help you.

There is too much that is not offered when you represent yourself. A paper mill that spews out documents is no substitute for real legal representation. How will you proceed with discovery or collection of evidence? Do you really want to be deposed for five hours without the benefit of legal experience?

You deprive yourself of essential knowledge of case law and basic requirements such as filing motions. It is difficult enough, with an attorney, to venture into the jungle of consumer protection and a virtual impossibility without one.

I always advise a wronged consumer retain legal counsel. This is not because I am attorney I am not. It is not because I like attorneys, I don't. Lawyers are a necessary evil in a bad world and that is the best I can say for them today. There is nothing good I can say for representing yourself in court any day.

Furthermore, loan rescue services have been recognized largely as scams. These lowlifes charge their victims thousands of dollars and offer no real help. The documents they produce are boilerplate form pleadings that when filed provide little or no protection and in fact put families at risk of losing their homes. This is because homeowners are not having experts really look at the facts on the ground and proceed accordingly on their behalf. Instead they believe a foreclosure rescue is performing this duty the next thing they know they are out of a house.

Regarding your inability to afford an attorney 1) if you have $2,500 to pay a document mill you have enough to retain an attorney for such services, 2) if you have no money look into legal aid in your area. For more information for legal aid in your area visit www.consumershock.org and click on resources.

In closing let me give you another bit of good consumer advice, when consuming legal goods or using an attorney, know what you're getting. Take notes; ask questions so you have an understanding of what is happening and why. Be sure you are content with your attorney and the services they provide.

Question 7

Question: Can you describe some of the housing programs created by the Bush and the Obama Administrations?

Answer: The housing collapse of recent years has produced a number of responses by both the Bush and Obama Administrations. The most common complaint about these programs is that they don't assist those who are unemployed or too far behind in payments. There are other shortfalls as well.

The Hope Now alliance initiated by the Bush team has proven to be severely limited in who can qualify. HOPE NOW was a joint effort by HUD approved counseling agents, mortgage companies, investors and other mortgage market participants to provide free foreclosure prevention assistance.

Created in 2007, proponents of the idea claim it has assisted 1 million homeowners. The objective was to allow folks to reach an agreement on a repayment schedule or if this was not possible a loan modification. The problem is it was left to the discretion of mortgage companies if they wanted to participate or not.

The Hope Now Program is recommending several loan programs. Project Lifeline targets homeowners that are delinquent 90-days or more. Six HOPE NOW alliance members that are servicers will begin the program by providing a letter to seriously delinquent homeowners offering a simple "step-by-step" approach that, if followed, may enable them to "pause" their foreclosure for 30 days while a potential loan modification is evaluated.

Project Lifeline includes only a half dozen of America's largest lenders more interested, as was the Bush Administration, in appearance than substance. This plan, like all the others offered by both the government and the banks, has been criticized as ineffective window dressing.

Another program offered by the Hope Now counselors is the HOPE for Homeowners (H4H) program that was created by Congress to help those at risk of default and foreclosure to refinance into more affordable, sustainable loans. The program will be in effect from October 1, 2008 through September 30, 2011. For borrowers who refinance under HOPE for Homeowners, lenders will be required to "write down" the size of the mortgage to a maximum of 90 percent of the home's new appraised value. HOPE for Homeowners will only offer 30-year, fixed rate mortgages. To qualify your mortgage must have originated on or before January 1, 2008.

The Federal Housing Authority's FHASecure program offers refinancing options to help delinquent ARM borrowers get reasonable, fixed-rate loans. FHASecure targets owners whose mortgages have gone delinquent due to the increase in payments after interest rates have reset. Since that doesn't happen for at least two years for most hybrid ARM loans, those written after December 31, 2006 will not qualify for the program.

The Making Home Affordable Program President Obama started will help you refinance if you are a homeowner who is current on your mortgage payments but unable to refinance to a lower interest rate because your home value has decreased. The most recent "foreclosure remedy" introduced by the new administration also offers more incentives to banks to become involved. If you are a homeowner who is current on your mortgage payments but unable to refinance to a lower interest rate because your home value has decreased, you may be able to refinance.

For a loan refinance:

- You must be the owner of a one- to four-unit home;
- You must be current on your mortgage payments; "Current" means that you haven't been more than 30-days late on your mortgage payment in the last 12 months;
- You believe that the amount you owe on your first mortgage is about the same or less than the current value of your house.

For a loan modification:

- They got a mortgage before January 1, 2009;

- Having trouble making payments on time;
- The amount you owe on your first mortgage equal to or less than $729,750;
- Payment on your first mortgage (including principal, interest, taxes, insurance and homeowner's association dues, if applicable) is more than 31% of your current gross income.

Many housing advocates believe these actions are still not as substantial as the foreclosure crisis demands. If you are too far behind in payments or your house has depreciated in value beyond the threshold then you don't qualify.

With the increase in unemployment and foreclosure threatening homeownership and the middleclass itself, more drastic measures may be needed. Many experts believe a foreclosure moratorium that suspends all foreclosures for six months or one year is needed to stop the snowball effect taking place.

Whether or not these programs will help remains to be seen. If you are waiting on any legislation aimed at curbing the majority of foreclosures to an absolute minimum; don't hold your breath. A complete overhaul as well as regulation of an irresponsible and corrupt banking system is required in order to save homeownership.

Question 8

Question: I have often wondered why it would take so long to pay off our mortgage. I have been told it has to do with amortization and my interest rate. What is loan amortization and how do I find out about it regarding my loan?

Answer: Amortization is a payment method where part of your monthly payment goes to pay toward the principal or borrowed amount and another part goes to paying the interest.

In the beginning of your payment plan the majority of your monthly payments will go toward interest payments and a very small portion toward the principal. This payment distribution continues for a number of years, approximately eighteen years of a 30-year mortgage, and then the majority of the payment goes towards satisfaction of the principal. The determining factor of when the greater part of your monthly payments goes toward your principal is based upon how much your interest rate is, or essentially how much you are paying for your loan.

Your bank should be providing information regarding the amortization of your loan with your monthly bill. Included in your bill should be an amortization schedule or table detailing what amount of your payments go to principal and interest.

Be sure your bank knows you have a right to your account information and provides accurate data regarding your amortization schedule. This will tell you how much has been paid-to-date and how much is owed for both principal and interest.

Amortization can have a borrower repaying 300%-500% of the original amount of the loan. Every time a homeowner refinances the entire process starts all over again with the amortizing payment plan. This is standard operating procedure and how banks really make their money from mortgages.

Keep your bank honest and check their math. In order to determine payment schedule do an Internet search for an amortization calculator. You will need to factor in the original amount borrowed, payment amount, interest rate, and number of payments you are required to make.

Question 9

Question: We have been renters for years and we are now considering buying. In the current market is this a good idea, let alone possible?

Answer: It is a buyers market because there is an excess of houses available and prices have plummeted. The problem is banks are not lending unless you have a pristine credit rating. You will need to have cash for the down payment and employment documentation. No money down and no documents required loans are a thing of the past, for now.

It would be best for you to avoid mortgage brokers of any kind. This way you can steer clear of high interest, high fee, and predatory loans. Bad bankers have been dealing out toxic loans for years. It is the failure of these mortgages that has crushed our economy.

As we revisit a national collapse we haven't seen since the 1930's, there is little or no effort to fix the problem that started it all, bad banking. There is no transparency in the banking world. The result is dangerous loan products that end in foreclosure. This is why you must be very careful in approaching homeownership.

In order to do so consult with a HUD approved housing counselor. Take the time go through the guidance process so that you understand HUD's nine steps to homeownership.

They are:

1. How much you can afford.
2. Understanding your rights.
3. How to shop for a mortgage.
4. Learn about particular loan programs.
5. How to shop for a home.
6. How to make an offer.
7. How to get a home inspection.
8. Shopping for homeowners insurance.
9. Understanding closing procedure and documents.

HUD is a great place for first time homeowners to learn the essential knowledge required in purchasing a home before jumping into a complex and oftentimes predatory market. FHA loan programs offer lower down payments and are a good option for first-time homebuyers; the Federal Housing Administration (FHA) has been part of HUD since 1965. Another bonus is you are provided a list of HUD approved lenders.

Contact HUD approved housing counselor
http://www.hud.gov

Question 10

Question: We are trying to refinance our mortgage to get a better rate that is fixed. Our bank will not work with us what should we do?

Answer: First, contact HUD regarding the FHASecure Program for homeowners with an adjustable rate mortgage or ARM. It would be a good idea to get signed up with a HUD-approved housing counselor before you make any other banking moves.

HUD offers a step-by-step understanding of the loan process and how to get the best mortgage possible. You can benefit by lower rates offered with their loan programs and HUD-approved lenders.

If push turns to shove and HUD cannot assist you in your endeavor you will have to contact lenders directly to see if you can refinance with them. As everyone is probably all too aware of in the current chaos of banking, it is difficult to get loans.

There are dangers you will need to avoid if you do get a loan. The best thing you can do to stay away from a bad loan is to have your own attorney handle the loan closing. This way you can have a transparent and understandable loan experience. Otherwise there is a good chance you will get an oppressive or predatory mortgage. It is essential you get the same loan at closing that you were promised.

There have been too many crooks and thugs in the banking business for far too long. I truly believe, given the opportunity, all creditors will abuse you. I have a sneaky suspicion that you couldn't swing a dead banker without hitting a bad mortgage. I would be surprised if there was not something wrong with your loan.

I am a big proponent of making sure your bank is doing everything correct and is following the law. If your bank does not want to work with you, be certain they have all their paperwork in order before they try to foreclose.

Making written requests for 1) the note, 2) the security instrument and 3) an itemized statement of your account can send your bank into a paralysis trying to produce the documents they must legally provide. Many times the lender cannot provide a security instrument and are at a loss to force a foreclosure.

If you have to file a civil suit against your mortgage company in order to bring your bank to a mediation table to modify your loan terms then so be it. Regardless of how unfriendly your bank becomes remember they have to follow the law. Don't let them run over you and don't let them run you out of your home.

To those scratching their heads and asking "wasn't this a question about refinancing?" All roads lead to a fight when you are dealing with banks.

Question 11

Question: How can I hire an attorney if I cannot afford one and what can I expect?

Answer: You need to contact legal aid in your area to see if you qualify for their services. Other options include legal assistance from local college or university law school programs and pro bono legal programs.

The steps described below usually take years to complete. In my own situation it took six years before it reached court.

- Once you have a lawyer the lender is no longer allowed to have any contact with you directly. All correspondence must be through your attorney.

- All collection actions are put on hold.

- Any violations are included in a proper complaint. This formal complaint is filed with a circuit or federal court and pursued as a civil suit.

- Once the complaint is filed in a court, the bad bankers will have approximately 30 days to respond.

- The first response by the offending lender is to deny any wrongdoing and to "paper" your attorney. This refers to a common process by which the defendant's legal team responds to the plaintiff's lawyer with a pile of papers. There will be several pages of answers to the allegations and several more pages of requests for statements of the facts and documentation of the wrongdoing. The documents collected will fill several boxes before it is over.

- All sides named in your lawsuit will give depositions. A deposition is testimony (outside of the courtroom) given under oath, detailing what has happened. You have not lived until you have been deposed by corporate lawyers asking you questions for four or five hours. It is like pulling teeth without the benefit of anesthesia, as legal weasels turn the question and answer phase into something medieval. Brace yourself for this, it can be punishing. Just remember these attorneys want to intimidate you; stick to your guns tell the truth and just let them know at every turn you expect to leave the case for a jury of your peers to decide and not you or anyone other than a jury, as a matter of being unbiased and fair.

- Your lawyer should make requests for 1) the note, 2) security instrument, 3) an itemized statement of your account and any other documents they have concerning your loan. This can send your bank into a paralysis trying to produce documents they must legally provide. Many times the lender cannot provide a security instrument and are at a loss to force a foreclosure.

- Most states would rather both parties reach an agreement by means of arbitration or negotiation. If all else fails, you have the right to appear in court and have a jury decide. You also have the right to not mediate at all, and insist upon a jury trial.

The majority of predatory loan situations reaching this point end in a settlement instead of a trial. This is determined by how willing your bank is to workout an amiable deal and how effective your attorney is in negotiating.

You can expect frustration with the amount time the process takes, the asinine things your bank will try and even the performance of your own lawyer. The end of the ordeal will leave you tired and beaten up; there will be no thought of victory, only one of survival.

For legal aid information in your area visit www.consumershock.org and click on resources.

Question 12

Question: Because of the recent adjustment in our mortgage payment it has become unaffordable overnight. There is no equity left in our house to refinance and the bank is not interested in working out a deal.

We have maxed-out all of our credit cards and have been forced into high fee, high interest, payday loans to get by. Furthermore, we have been notified that a service has been hired to repossess our two cars.

What can we do to avoid foreclosure and the loss of our vehicles?

Answer: I don't believe it will be possible for you to avoid a series of consumer shocks in coming months. Whether these will be jolts or catastrophic life-changing events are really up to you. A lot of unpleasant realities need to be confronted head on.

For starters you need to decide what degree of debt you can realistically or comfortably maintain. The amount of debt you are currently laboring under sounds like far too much of a burden. Two things are obvious; you have escalated beyond your means and you are oblivious to how bad of a situation you are in.

I assume if you could have entered into a payment plan with your creditors you would have and this has proven impossible. Is it possible to shed a new car or two and workout a deal to save your home? If you have a repossession company looking for your cars then you need to turn them into the lot you bought them from and buy a used car or consider taking the bus for a while; there is always the "shoe leather express."

Your mortgage situation may prove far more painful than the car extractions. Contact HUD to be assigned a housing counselor that could propose alternatives to foreclosure. If you are too far behind in payments and/or unemployed, recent programs put in place may be no assistance to you.

Check with HUD about the FHASecure Program if your mortgage payments have changed because of a adjustable rate mortgage or ARM.

With the recent changes in bankruptcy law, you may find some protections under Chapter 13. New rules allow the judge to modify the terms of a mortgage so homeowners can keep their houses. Unfortunately, the changes do not help those who are jobless.

Making written requests for 1) the note, 2) the security instrument and 3) an itemized statement of your account can send your bank into a paralysis trying to produce documents they must legally provide. Many times the lender cannot provide a security instrument and are at a loss to force a foreclosure.

There is always the option of filing a civil suit to make your bank produce all the required documentation above. If you have any experiences that have been abusive or have received a loan quite different from the one you thought you were getting, then you need an attorney.

There are no easy ways out or quick fixes. If there is a possibility of saving your home you will have a tough fight ahead of you. Fighting for your home may not save it but it can "buy you time", oftentimes years, to set aside enough money to move into a rental. This is possible because filing a civil suit suspends your bank's ability to collect.

The era of too much credit card debt has come to an end. The difficult times we find ourselves in demands critical thinking by all consumers regarding their ability to maintain debt. Too many cars, too much house, and too little financial planning will end in a disaster.

Contact a local, HUD-approved housing counseling agency at HUD.gov

Visit www.consumershock.org click on resources for legal aid info in your area.

www.ingramcontent.com/pod-product-compliance
Lightning Source LLC
Chambersburg PA
CBHW022013170526
45157CB00003B/1228